BRIGHT
IDEAS
BOOKS

AMAZING
Lakes
AROUND
THE WORLD

by Roxanne Troup

raintree
a Capstone company — publishers for children

Raintree is an imprint of Capstone Global Library Limited, a company incorporated in England and Wales having its registered office at 264 Banbury Road, Oxford, OX2 7DY – Registered company number: 6695582

www.raintree.co.uk
myorders@raintree.co.uk

Text © Capstone Global Library Limited 2020
The moral rights of the proprietor have been asserted.

All rights reserved. No part of this publication may be reproduced in any form or by any means (including photocopying or storing it in any medium by electronic means and whether or not transiently or incidentally to some other use of this publication) without the written permission of the copyright owner, except in accordance with the provisions of the Copyright, Designs and Patents Act 1988 or under the terms of a licence issued by the Copyright Licensing Agency, Barnard's Inn, 86 Fetter Lane, London, EC4A 1EN (www.cla.co.uk). Applications for the copyright owner's written permission should be addressed to the publisher.

Edited by Claire Vanden Branden
Designed by Becky Daum
Original illustrations © Capstone Global Library Limited 2020
Production by Dan Peluso

ISBN 978 1 4747 7464 2 (hardback)
ISBN 978 1 4747 8117 6 (paperback)

British Library Cataloguing in Publication Data
A full catalogue record for this book is available from the British Library.

Acknowledgements
We would like to thank the following for permission to reproduce photographs: iStockphoto: CampPhoto, 13, 28, dtokar, 26–27, fdastudillo, 14–15, herreid, 7, jskiba, 8–9, Rafael_Wiedenmeier, 17, RuslanDashinsky, 25, simonbradfield, 5; Shutterstock Images: Elnur, 18–19, insideout78, 21, Rafal Cichawa, 22–23, topseller, cover, withGod, 11, 31

Every effort has been made to contact copyright holders of material reproduced in this book. Any omissions will be rectified in subsequent printings if notice is given to the publisher.

All the internet addresses (URLs) given in this book were valid at the time of going to press. However, due to the dynamic nature of the internet, some addresses may have changed, or sites may have changed or ceased to exist since publication. While the author and publisher regret any inconvenience this may cause readers, no responsibility for any such changes can be accepted by either the author or the publisher.

CONTENTS

CHAPTER 1

AMAZING
Lakes

Lakes are bodies of water that fill low areas. Most contain fresh water, but some are made up of salt water. All lakes are surrounded by land. Some lakes are huge and others are very small.

Lakes can have many amazing features. Some lakes have fish as big as people. Other lakes even have sharks. Some lakes are pink. Other lakes change colour. Discover some of the world's most amazing lakes.

There are more than 115 million lakes on Earth.

CHAPTER 2

THE GREAT
Lakes

The Great Lakes are the biggest lakes in North America. These connected lakes cover more of the world than any other lake.

There are five Great Lakes. Lake Superior is the largest. Lake Ontario is the smallest.

The five Great Lakes are Lake Huron, Lake Ontario, Lake Michigan, Lake Erie and Lake Superior (below).

The Great Lakes act like small oceans.

Their waves can be 9 metres (30 feet) high.

They have more than 35,000 islands.

Some of the lakes are full of sturgeon.

These fish can grow to be as big as an

adult human.

In the past, lighthouses along the shores of the Great Lakes were necessary to guide ships.

CHAPTER 3

LAKE
Baikal

Lake Baikal is in Russia. It is the oldest lake on Earth. It is also the world's deepest lake. It is more than 1.6 kilometres (1 mile) deep.

The lake is home to unusual animals.

One of these animals is the Baikal seal.

Baikal seals are the world's smallest seals.

They live in fresh water. They can only be

found in Lake Baikal.

More than 80,000 Baikal seals live in Lake Baikal.

CHAPTER 4

CRATER
Lake

Crater Lake formed in the **crater** of a volcano. It is in Oregon, USA. It is the deepest lake in the United States. More than 750,000 people visit the lake each year.

LAKE TAHOE

Lake Tahoe is the second deepest lake in the United States. It is between Nevada and California.

Wizard's Island is in the middle of Crater Lake.

An old tree stump floats in the lake. It has been floating for more than 100 years. It has been given the name Old Man of the Lake.

CHANGING COLOURS

The Kelimutu Lakes are crater lakes in Indonesia. Scientists believe gases from the volcano change the colour of the lake. It can be blue, green, red or black.

Scientists believe Old Man of the Lake is at least 450 years old.

CHAPTER 5

THE CASPIAN
Sea

The Caspian Sea is in the Middle East. It is a large salty lake. It used to be part of the ocean. But now it is surrounded by land.

The Caspian Sea is called a sea because of its size and salt water. But many scientists also call it a lake.

HUGE LAKE

The Caspian Sea covers 370,368 square kilometres (143,000 square miles). It is the largest lake in the world. It is rich in oil and natural gas.

Oil rigs drill for oil in the Caspian Sea.

CHAPTER 6

LAKE
Titicaca

Lake Titicaca is in South America. It is called the birthplace of the Incan people. But **ruins** in the area are older than the Incas.

Lake Titicaca is on the border of Peru and Bolivia.

THE UROS PEOPLE

The Uros people have lived on Lake Titicaca for 3,000 years. They were there long before the Incas. The Uros didn't want to fight the Incas, so they used **reeds** to build islands to escape. They have lived on these islands ever since.

FRESHWATER SHARKS

Lake Nicaragua is the largest lake in Central America. It has fresh water, but it is full of sharks! Sharks usually live in the ocean.

The reed islands the Uros people live on are known as floating islands.

23

CHAPTER 7

THE DEAD Sea

The Dead Sea is in Israel. It is sometimes called the Salt Sea. This lake is saltier than the ocean. It is so salty that people can't swim. They float instead!

The Dead Sea is up to 10 times saltier than the ocean.

Minerals from the Dead Sea are used all over the world. Some of these minerals are used to make skin care products.

PINK LAKE

Lake Hiller is a salt lake in Australia. The water is pink. This colour comes from **algae** in the lake.

Only **bacteria** can live in the Dead Sea.

GLOSSARY

algae
very small organisms that grow from plants in water and are usually green

bacteria
tiny living things that exist everywhere in nature

crater
opening at the top of a volcano

mineral
natural material that doesn't come from plants or animals

reed
tall, long grass that grows near water

ruins
remains of an old civilization

TOP
LAKES
TO VISIT

CASPIAN SEA, MIDDLE EAST
   Take a trip to the largest lake in the world.

CRATER LAKE, OREGON, USA
   Travel to this lake in the crater of a volcano.

DEAD SEA, ISRAEL
   Enjoy this natural spa as you float in the saltiest lake
on Earth.

GREAT LAKES, USA
   Visit the largest area of fresh water on Earth.

LAKE BAIKAL, RUSSIA
   Explore the oldest lake on the planet.

LAKE NICARAGUA, NICARAGUA
   See this freshwater lake filled with sharks.

LAKE TITICACA, PERU AND BOLIVIA
   Come to the home of the Uros people and their
floating islands.

ACTIVITY

FIND OUT MORE!

Pretend you are visiting one of the amazing lakes in this book. What would you ask the people who live near that lake? For example, when is the best time of year to visit the lake? What activities are there to do on the lake? What part of the lake is the most popular to visit?

Research the answers to your questions. Then write a short summary of what you have learned. After your research, which lake interests you the most?

FIND OUT MORE

Books

DKfindout! Earth, DK (DK Children, 2017)

Earth's Landforms (Earth By Numbers), Nancy Dickmann (Raintree, 2018)

The World's Most Amazing Lakes (Landform Top Tens), Michael Hurley (Ralntree, 2010)

Websites

www.bbc.com/bitesize/articles/zvys8xs

Explore the Lake District!

www.dkfindout.com/uk/earth/rivers/how-does-an-oxbow-lake-form

Find out how an oxbow lake is formed.

INDEX